WHAT!
Do you think
GOD
hates you?

W D Taylor

WestBow
PRESS
A DIVISION OF THOMAS NELSON

WestBow Press books may be ordered through booksellers or by contacting:

WestBow Press
A Division of Thomas Nelson
1663 Liberty Drive
Bloomington, IN 47403
www.westbowpress.com
1-(866) 928-1240

ISBN: 978-1-4908-0606-8 (sc)
ISBN: 978-1-4908-0607-5 (hc)
ISBN: 978-1-4908-0605-1 (e)

Library of Congress Control Number: 2013915282

Printed in the United States of America.

WestBow Press rev. date: 11/04/2013

Introduction

I THOUGHT IT NECESSARY TO PUT into writing why so many people think God hates them. I was on my bed and sleep didn't come, so I prayed all night until about three in the morning. Then I asked God if I could have some sleep, and I told him I would start on this book in the morning. From time to time this will happen to me: I'll start praying, and time will fly by, hour by hour. This time I didn't mind it too much because I was out of work, my truck was broken down, and I didn't have much to do the next day except spend some money on my old truck. The motor needed to be rebuilt, so I would have to repair it . . . not that I wanted to (junkyard, here I come).

Many of us know what it's like to struggle. Life has a way of beating us down, and God has a way of lifting us up. Many books have been written on subjects like this, but they often fail to tell us why we go through so many struggles from time to time—more often than not, it seems. In other words, why doesn't God do something about my situation, problems, troubles, pains, losses, and so on?

This book is dedicated to my mother, whom I lost to cancer some time ago. Ever since, I have set out to be a thorn in Satan's side and to reveal the liar he really is. God's passion to see all human beings saved has led me to see the need for people of all nations to come to God and repent of their sins and call on the name of Jesus Christ for forgiveness and salvation. It is my heart's desire that you would see how great a love God has for you.

Contents

1

My Life So Far

I was born in a small town just north of Destin, Florida. I was ten pounds, one ounce. My mother was fifteen years old when I was born. I was not a small child, and she has had a hard life from the day she was born, which could be another book by itself. My dad was a young man; Mother was his second or third marriage. He has had many losses; he lost a child at birth, and he lost a child in a divorce when he gave up my older brother to adoption.

I can say that my mom and dad loved me and my little sister very much. Even now as I look back at all those pictures and remember all the hard times they had, I can say we had some good times and bad times, to say the least. But that is common with most families.

I grew up on an old country road in a small house with a young mother and a dad; well, let's just say he would have a beer from time to time. The times he was not drinking, he was the best dad a child could ask for. I have poured out many beer cans. Drinking changes a man, you know; I have seen it firsthand. My mom has since passed away; in other words, she is with the Lord Jesus Christ, our Savior. My dad is still with us here on earth, an old man still working hard every day, as he always has.

My grandmother on my dad's side was what most people in the South would call a churchgoer. My dad was a deacon in the church before I was born, but I have only seen him in church one time in my whole life. My grandmother would come pick us up and take my little sister and me to church with her on Sunday mornings. I remember she had one of those bobble head dogs in the back glass of her car, and she would give us gum to keep us quiet during church services. After church, it was ice cream. My grandmother was a storekeeper, and the store was next to the old church. We got all the Cokes we could drink—they came in glass bottles—and my favorite Golden Flakes potato chips and all the strawberry ice cream we wanted. But that wasn't why I loved her so much; no, it was because she was the best grandmother a grandson could have had. She was very picky, so her house was always clean; everything had its place. She would give me a bath in her bathroom sink. I remember her telling me, "You have to make sure to wash behind your ears before you go to bed." They must have been very dirty. Let's face it; I was a boy, and boy did I love to play! I was always into something living in the country.

One afternoon when we got out of church, I was in a hurry to get my ice cream. My grandmother was older and slow, so I ran on ahead. I'll never forget doing this. I got to the old country store in the back and kicked the door so many times that I kicked a hole in her back door. I must have been a brat. She never screamed at me. All she said was, "Son, you shouldn't do things like that." And after all that I had done, she still gave me my ice cream. After all these years I still remember doing that, and now I wish I would have helped her down that sandy dirt road we walked after church on Sunday. Some grandchild I was.

I didn't know my granddad, and I don't know much about him except that he was a hard worker. I know he owned a dairy farm and a store, none of which came easy.

My grandmother went to be with the Lord Jesus Christ, her Savior, when I was eleven years old. It was a sad time for me. I love her very much, and even today it still breaks my heart.

If it weren't for my grandmother, I wouldn't have gotten saved. I remember sitting in the back of the church with her before she died. I don't remember why we were sitting there, because we always sat in the front. Anyway, the preacher must have been preaching a good sermon, as the Holy Spirit was moving. He touched my heart that day, and when the invitation was given, I was scared to death. I wasn't about to get up in front of all of those people, as that wasn't like me. However, this was different. Before I knew it, I was looking at everybody, and not from behind. I was face to face with the whole congregation. Jesus Christ saved me that day. The Holy Spirit must have picked me up, because I don't remember walking to the front of that church. I am thankful that my grandmother cared enough to take time out of her day to come to our house and get us for church.

I remember telling that preacher I was going home and was going to read the whole Bible, even though I couldn't read. They told me I was slow. I spent two years in kindergarten, two years in first grade, and two years in third grade. At that rate, I figured I'd be a grown man by the time I was in junior high. Mom finally moved us to another school. I passed the fourth grade, they passed me from the fifth grade to the seventh grade, and I passed the seventh grade; in eighth grade, we moved back to the old school, and I started failing again. I quit school in the ninth grade and got a job. I was sixteen and thought I was smarter than everybody else.

Anyway, I remember my dad picking me up after church that day. I told him what had happened, that I got saved that day. I'll never forget what he said: "What did you do that for?" I thought he would have been happy for me; maybe he was and wished he had been there for me. I don't know what was so important that he wasn't in church. I do know he had been drinking, like most of the time. I know that whatever it was couldn't have been more important than seeing his child ask Jesus Christ to save him.

At this point, things didn't get any better. I still lived in the same world, in the same home, with same parents, and with the same people doing the same things.

After my grandmother died, I didn't get to church anymore for some time. It's kind of like the old saying goes: you take a pig, clean it up, and bring it inside, but as soon as you put it back in the pig pin, it will play in the mud. That sums up my teenage years: I was saved but playing in the mud.

The next few years were spent moving from town to town, house to house. Mom moved us every few months, trying to hide from our dad. They got divorced when I was young. I had many stepmoms and stepdads.

I've seen many fights between my parents— I've even seen my dad hit my mom. He hit her so hard one night she fell and hit her head on a doorknob, and the whole side of her head was black and blue. We would try to stay out of his way as much as possible.

Once when I was about sixteen or so, my dad had been drinking a few beers, and I wanted to go to the gym to work out. He had a girlfriend or wife at the time; I don't think he had married this one, though I don't know for sure and didn't really want to call and ask him. Anyway, she didn't want me to leave, so she started in on him.

She told my dad not to let me leave. One thing led to the other, and by the time we were done, he had tried to cut me as I was holding him down by the front porch. I then tried to run to the car to get away, but he was right behind me with some kind of stick. As I got to the car, there wasn't time to get away. He tried to hit me, but I ducked. He missed, and the fight was on. Later he tried to shoot me with the same shotgun his dad had tried to shoot him with. This was all because he had been drinking and some woman was trying to play Mom. Sadly, I broke my dad's ribs in the fight. I remember hitting him so many times, and every time I would hit him, I would say, "This is for Momma, for my sister, and for me." I was put in a bad spot no son should ever be in. Never the less, I was there fighting with my dad. I should have just stayed or let him beat me, but I have to live with that. Now I was on my own; I never lived with my dad again.

It took some time, but we eventually got past those years and the fight. He loves me, and I love him. I wouldn't take another dad if God gave me one. He's a good man who had a hard time, and I believe he did what he thought was best at that time.

Another example of my "playing in the mud" was when I ran away from home one time. My stepbrother and I were found in the swamps of Florida, growing marijuana. It was meant to be a get-rich-quick scheme, but we were caught when I was about fifteen, and they put us in jail. We weren't in for very long; it was just a little slap on the hand. *That* really worked.

When I got out, I started stealing. We stole all kind of things; you would be surprised at what most people would buy. We would steal from one man to sell to another businessman. I would watch the police to see where they were, and I would go to work, stealing anything not nailed down—guns, cars, trucks, jewelry, lawn movers, and gas. I even took oil out of someone's truck one night. Like I said, if it wasn't nailed down, it was gone.

My mom and I stole a truck one night. She ran spot, and I drove the stolen truck to a well-known businessman in a town close to where we lived. He had a chop shop and rebuilt a lot of trucks for the fine, outstanding citizens of our small town. He also had some of the cops paid off.

My dad, a friend of his, and I tried stealing a hog one night. I drove the getaway car. We didn't get the hog. They shot one that was too big to put into the trunk of a Chevy Nova. I also remember my dad telling me how to hide stolen car parts left over in fishponds and lakes.

There's a lot a parent can teach a child, and my mom and dad taught me how to take what didn't belong to me. A job would have been easier. I never worked so hard in my life as I did when I was trying to avoid getting caught by the owners and cops.

However, I got caught anyway, for breaking into a shopping mall. I thought I was so smart. We went in through the roof, missed the jewelry store by one room. Next door was a sewing machine store, and I couldn't sell sewing machines. So we knocked a hole through the wall to get into the jewelry store, but we didn't know there was a hair salon behind the jewelry store, so we had to knock another hole through the wall of the jewelry store. Talk about work! And talk about being hardheaded!

I went to prison that time and found out man was not meant to sit in a cage like a dog. But that was one of the best things God could have ever let happen to me. At the time this seemed like a *tragedy* to my family and me. I was on a road of no return, and a bank was in the works—who knows how far I would have gone? Only God knows our heart and how to get our attention, and he had mine!

I remember praying one night in prison. I said, "Lord, when I get out of here, I want a wife who will keep me off of drugs." By drugs, I mean marijuana and alcohol. I never did any of that other junk; marijuana and alcohol were bad enough. I said she doesn't have to be pretty, but I don't want a ugly wife either. And boy did he know just what I would like: black headed and feisty. I also said I don't want to be rich, but I don't want to be poor either. Boy, I should have thought on that one a little more. Anyway I told him that I didn't want my children to be fat; I am fat, my mom was fat, and we hated being fat. I didn't want my children to go through what we had to go through. None of my children are overweight; in fact, they are skinny, and they hate it. Who knew? I told God that if he would do this for me, I would teach my children who he is and about his only begotten Son, Jesus Christ, my Savior, and he answered my prayer to a tee. Any of my children will tell you without hesitation that Jesus Christ is God and has saved them. God gave me my family, and I thank him for each one of them; that makes me one of the richest men on earth. One thing you can count on is God always keeps his word, and he knows your heart and if you keep your word. God is all knowing.

Eventually I became an electrician. I even started my own electrical company in Wisconsin called ARK Electric, named after Noah's ark. I also started building houses in Wisconsin, Florida, and Kentucky, my wife pushing me the whole way. I always say that behind every good man is an equally good woman.

In Genesis 2:18, God said he would make Adam a "help meet," and he made mine for me. I tried to stay home with my family as much as possible but had to take other jobs from time to time when things got slow. God knows how to reach the lost and he was using me.

I always found that God had someone who needed to hear the gospel of Jesus Christ, and then he would move me on. I thank God for every opportunity he has given me to witness for him. For as long as I can remember, I have had a heart to see people get saved. See, I know what it means to be lost and in need of a Savior.

My wife and I have had our share of hard times. However, the good times always outweigh the bad. Aside from a wonderful wife, I have kids and grandkids, and we are just getting started, thanks to God. Without him, we wouldn't even be here.

My kids are all grown up now and doing well. They have their share of struggles just like everybody else, but that is what makes us who we are. It's just like what I always say to those who will listen: your trials, sufferings, and losses will do one of two things; they will drive you to God or away from God, and you will either blame God, or you will praise him. It's just that way. As for me, I will fall on my knees and ask God to please help me, and he always does.

As the Bible says,

> And I say unto you, ask and it shall be given you; seek and ye shall find; knock, and it shall be opened unto you. For every one that asketh receiveth; and he that seeketh findeth and to him that knocketh it shall be opened. If a son shall ask for bread of any of you that is a Father, will he give him a stone? Or if he asks a fish, will he for a fish give him a serpent? Or if he shall ask an egg, will he offer him a scorpion? If they, being evil, know how to give good gifts unto your children: how

14

much more shall your heavenly Father give the Holy Spirit to them that ask him? (Luke 11:9-13)KJV

God is good all the time.

Peoples Foolish Ideas

HUMANKIND HAS, AS LONG AS I can tell, tried to find the origin of life. Humankind has spent more of its resources looking for signs of life in places that don't make any sense. They have looked everywhere they can go and have tried everything they can think of to do; God will allow us only to go so far.

The United States has spent billions of dollars funding the National Aeronautics and Space Administration, better known as NASA. In 2001, the United States sent the Odyssey, a robotic spacecraft, to orbit Mars. And why would the United States do something like that? Some believe Mars holds the answer to the origin of life and is thought to be a prime target for human colonization. What's next? Maybe they will try to go to the sun. And surprise! That is just what they are trying to do. NASA has decided to go to the sun in 2018; the mission is called Solar Probe Plus. (I hope they schedule it for a night mission.) Do we need more water? Or maybe we are in short supply of radiation? Have we overpopulated the earth? Maybe they are thinking that if we destroy the earth as we know it with all our nuclear bombs, we could live on Mars. Or it could be they are just looking for signs of life. Let's say they do find signs of life on some distant planet; that doesn't change anything. God is still God, and we are still just people wasting time and resources on our foolish ideas. Just how far we will go is yet to be seen. Today much of the world sees evolution as the source of life: something from nothing. The best of the best has to beat out the rest. Boy, do we have a long way to go with ideas like that. The man who came up with the theory of evolution that is so popular today is dead. He has joined many elite scientists who have failed in their attempt to give an answer to the origin of life. That is only found right here on earth and in the word of God in the Bible, especially the book of Genesis, chapter one. Look what God said in 1 Corinthians 3:18-20: "Let no man deceive himself. If any man among you seemeth to be wise in this world, let him become a fool, that he may be wise for the wisdom of this world is foolishness to God for it is written, He taketh the wise in their own craftiness and again the Lord knoweth the thoughts of the wise that they are vain."

At one time, human beings thought the earth to be flat, and they believed the sun revolved around the earth and that the big bang was the beginning of our little space. The man who came up with evolution said, "Light will be thrown on the origin of man." Our origin is God who made Adam and Eve. This man suffered loss just like anyone else, including heart disease, the loss of children, and the loss of life physically and spiritually. He was critical of God's Word, and he thought all religions equally valid.

I often wonder if the people who thought the earth was flat ever wondered how the water stayed in place or if there was a bottom side of the earth. And if so, how would they get there? And would they fall off? Who would have thought back then they had it all wrong? They would have known if they had read the Bible.

In Isaiah 40:22, the Bible tells us, "It is He [God] that sitteth upon the circle of the earth, and the inhabitants thereof are as grasshoppers; that stretcheth out the heavens as a curtain and spreadth them out as a tent to dwell in." Yet today there are still some who believe that they evolved from monkeys of some kind. Humankind still thinks it can find the origin of life in a laboratory. At one time, humankind believed in spontaneous generation, which was disproved by biogenesis. I could have saved them some time! Just take the *bio* off of *biogenesis*, and you will have it (*Genesis*). The Greeks believed that living organisms could spontaneously come into being from nonliving matter. This theory has long been held by many in the world—even up to the present time. The law of biogenesis states that life arises from preexisting life. I would ask then: what preexisting life are they talking about? Some still think all you need to spark life is a little warm pond; I don't know about you, but I'll bet you that won't work either. Still, the argument goes on, and scientists will continue to reject God's Word or that there even is a God who created everything they are studying in creation.

Many people believe in the big bang theory. If that is how it all started, who caused that to happen? They can believe 13 billion years ago there was a big bang and the universe was born and expanded rapidly. That sounds logical? Yeah, right. What if they are wrong, and about six thousand years ago *God* spoke, and everything that was created came into being because he said so? Here is the problem with scientists: they rely on their own foolish assumptions. God said in Job 38:4,: Where wast thou when I laid the foundations of the earth? Declare, if thou hast understanding."

You might be thinking, well okay, where is your proof for God? I am glad you asked. The first thing to consider is yourself. Think about it for a moment: do you really think that something so complicated as yourself could really just come from nothing or that over billions of years you just started breathing air? And don't forget, it supposedly all just spontaneously appeared. The fact is that at some time in your life, you thought to yourself that there must be something out there that made all of this.

Look at Romans 1:19-21, "Because that which may be known of God is manifest in them; for God hath shewed it unto them. For the invisible things of him from the creation of the world are clearly seen, being understood by the things that are made, even his eternal power and Godhead; so that they are without excuse: because that, when they knew God, they glorified him not as God, neither were thankful; but became vain in their imagination, and their foolish heart was darkened." The problem I face in trying to convince you of God's existence is this question: how dark is your heart? Is it too late for you? Think of it this way. One day you will die. You might not want to. Never the less, you will die, and nothing you can do will change that fact.

In Genesis 3:19, the Bible tells us, "For dust thou art and unto dust shalt thou return. God is the creator and nothing you can do can change that fact either. Everything owes its existence to God and light has been thrown on the origin of life, that light is Jesus Christ our Lord and Savior." John 1:1-5 says, "In the beginning was the Word and the Word was with God and the Word was God the same was in the beginning with God all things were made by him and without him was not anything made that was made in him was life and the life was the light of men and the light shineth in darkness; and the darkness comprehended it not."

You cannot disprove that there is a God. No matter what you think or wish, you will not change the fact that there is a God. Way down deep inside you, you know there is a God. If you are at the point of no return, that is a tragedy of the worst kind: you are lost and separated from God because of the sin of unbelief.

Things That Seem Like Tragedies or Losses

IN THIS LIFE, IT SEEMS AS if there is no shortage of tragedies or losses. All over the world we see wars, people dying, hunger, sickness, loss of jobs, and divorce, and the list goes on and on. The one loss that sticks out in my mind the most is the hatred humankind has toward God. This is the one tragedy we cannot let destroy us.

Too many people have turned their backs on God. Unbelief is the one tragedy that will cost us more than any of us can afford to lose. What God is going to do with humankind is yet to be seen. Well, with most of them. However, that day is coming, and no one knows exactly when, but never the less it will come, and too many will perish. They will lose their souls and be forever forgotten. Everywhere you look, past or present, there is a so-called religion. Too many of us have fallen into the lie that all religions lead to God. In other words, we all believe in God, some say, but we just call him by other names. This is just not true! How can we all be right? God said in Matthew 7:13-14, "Enter ye in at the strait gate for wide is the gate, and broad is the way that leadeth to destruction, and many there be which go there at because strait is the gate and narrow is the way which leadeth unto life and few there be that find it." And in Proverbs 16:25, the Bible says, "There is a way that seemeth right unto a man but the ends thereof are the ways of death."

All religions are not right, and most of them are wrong. Let's face it; some will have to die to find out if God is real or not. Then it will be too late. Let's face another fact. We all will stand before God one day, and he will have to do something with each one of us based on one thing: Jesus Christ is his only begotten Son, who shed his blood on a cross publicly for all to see. How great a price God paid for each one of us that we may have life everlasting. If we would only ask God to forgive us of our own sins, the sins that separate us from him! For if we find ourselves standing before him not covered in that precious blood and with a heart of unbelief, he will have only one thing he can do with us. That will be total separation forever. Some he will let into heaven because of one thing: when he sees them, he will see the blood of Jesus Christ, his Son, and not their sins. But for way too many, he will see those sins that they cannot hide, and he will cast them into the lake of fire. The question is what will he do with you? Don't worry about me or anyone else; we have to answer for ourselves. You need to ask yourself, what if there is a God and you don't really know him? What if what this guy is saying is true, and I am wrong?

The loss of a child . . . I just can't imagine how hard it would be to try to make sense out of such a tragedy as that, or of a child who has a disease like cancer or AIDS. It seems as if a loss of this nature just is not fair to us. But we have to remember God never said life on earth would be fair. Jesus said in John 16:33, "These things I have spoken to you, that in me ye might have peace. In the world ye shall have tribulation; but be of good cheer, I have overcome the world."

The loss of my grandmother was hard for me to take as a young child. I didn't understand why she had to die. She was one of the best things in my life, and I would miss her very much. I think of her often. She has had a big influence on my life. I keep a picture of her on my desk. I was older when my granny died on my mother's side. Her death didn't hit me as my dad's mother did. This time it was harder. See, I was older and understood the loss they were going through. I watched my mother and her side of the family cry over the loss of their mother. As they tried to make sense out of her death, I'm sure this seemed like a tragedy to them.

Granny was a good woman, but like many of us, she was tired. In the hospital, she told me, "Son, I am ready to go. I have lived a long life, and I am tired. I am ready to go to heaven to be with God." I believe she was saved by the blood of Jesus Christ, our Lord and Savior, and is in heaven today.

Sometimes we have to ask the hard questions, the ones we try to forget about and hope we will never have to face, such as "Granny, are you saved? Will you go to heaven or hell?" You might be thinking that's too harsh, and I would tell you no, it is not! You're just a coward and afraid to ask. Letting your loved one die and not giving them one last chance to ask Jesus to save them is a tragedy. You have to make sure! Who knows? God might have put you in that place for that very purpose. When you die, it is too late to get saved. You have had your time on earth to ask and seek God. Don't take a chance on what some believe about purgatory. The prayers of loved ones can't help you when you die. Remember the story Jesus told about the certain rich man and the beggar named Lazarus in Luke 16:19?

There was a certain rich man, which was clothed in purple and fine linen, and fared sumptuously every day; And there was a certain begger named Lazarus, which laid at his gate, full of sores, and desiring to be fed with the crumbs which fell from the rich man's table; moreover the dogs came and licked his sores. And it came to pass, that the begger died and was carried by the angels into Abraham's bosom: The rich man also died and was buried; and in Hell he lifted up his eyes, being in torments, and seeth Abraham afar off and Lazarus in his bosom. And cried and said Father Abraham, have mercy on me and send Lazarus, that he may dip the tip of his finger in water, and cool my tongue; for I am tormented in this flame. But Abraham said Son, remember that thou in thy life time receivedst thy good things and Lazarus evil things; But now he is comforted and thou art tormented. And beside all of this, between us and you there is a great gulf fixed, so that they which would pass from you cannot, neither can they pass to you.

When I lost my mother to cancer, I had to be strong for my brother and sister. This was a very hard time for us. Even after a few years, it is still hard for me to take. The one thing that has held me together is the fact that my mother was saved. I knew God was going to take care of everything. No matter how hard I tried, this was one thing I could not fix. She was going to die, and it was killing me inside—just breaking my heart. The whole time, God would remind me of Matthew 10:37: "He that loveth father or mother more than me is not worthy of me and he that loveth son or daughter more than me is not worthy of me."

31

God gave me peace in the storm in the way that only he could do. God had given me time with mother before we knew she was sick. I moved back to Florida for a few years. I saw my mother smoking cigarettes and pot and drinking alcohol. She also lived with three different men. I remember the time I had to go and get her out of one of the local bars in Florida. She had gotten so drunk she could hardly walk. They called me and said I needed to come and get her because she was starting fights, and they were going to call the law if I didn't come and take her home.

I remember talking with my granny one day by the fence next to my mother's old house; my mother's sister was living there at the time with my mom's ex-husband. I said, "She is so embarrassing to me."

Granny didn't miss a beat; she said, "Son, she's doing the best she can do." See, Granny knew all too well about struggles. Now as I look back on my own life, I know I have embarrassed my mother more than one time.

I told my mother one time, "I sure wish you would stop smoking."

She said, "Well, son, I can't do that."

I said, "Just ask Jesus, and he will help you."

She said, "I am not going to do that."

I asked why not, and she said, "Because I know he will take it away."

At least she told the truth. She told me she would rather smoke than eat, and we loved to eat. It was hard for her to stop smoking. A few years later, she told me that God had made her so sick one day that she just quit. But it was too late, as we found out later in her life.

My mother did get saved before she died. What a tragedy it would have been if she had died not knowing Jesus Christ as her Savior. I tell you this because who knows? You might be able to help someone in your own family. Think about those of your own family; just think about it. Who do you want to see if you get to be with the Lord Jesus Christ? Will you be there? Or will they be there?

I was at this couple's house not long ago, giving a price on some work they needed done. After

talking with the man of the house, I found out
they had lost a grandchild who had been living
with them for some time. She was a teenager;
one day she was fine, and ten days later, she was
dead. They took her death hard. He quit his job,
and as far as I could tell, he just stayed around
the house. He seemed very sad to me. They had
kept everything she ever owned. It was piled
up to the ceiling. So after finding this out, you
know what I did. I wanted to ask the question
to try to encourage him and lift his spirits some;
besides, he still had a lot to be thankful for. His
other children and grandchildren were still alive
and in need of his guidance and love. As I said,
he had a lot to be thankful for. Besides all that,
he had told me he was saved. So I said, "Was she
saved?" and I'll never forget what that man said.
He said, "*I don't know.*" Well, I thought *what? You
don't know? How could you not know? What do you
mean you don't know?*

That was a tragedy to me, not knowing. No
wonder the man was so sad; it was amazing to
me he could even speak. How could anyone not

know if his grandchild was saved or not? This was someone who said he was saved, but he didn't know if his grandchild was. This is just what I mean by a true tragedy; this child could be in hell right now because someone didn't make sure. At least they could have asked her, "Honey, are you saved?" See, that's not so hard. At least they would have had some peace of mind knowing and not wondering.

Often losses happen when we least expect them. We think *that will not happen to me. Stuff like that only happen to other people.* Most people take too many chances with the life God gives them, such as driving drunk or talking on the phone while driving, to name a few. We are too careless; we just can't be careful enough.

My wife, from time to time, will tell the story about her grandfather, how he was a mail carrier in the horse and buggy days. He was riding down the road when a little girl ran after her ball, and he hit her, killing her on the spot. What a tragedy that was! Next came the part where he carried the little girl up to the home of the parents. Can you imagine having to do that? And what about those poor parents? I am sure all kinds of thoughts crossed their minds, that they should have done this or that. But it didn't matter anymore. It was too late. She was dead. The thing that stands out the most in this story to me is that no one in the story did anything wrong: he was carrying the mail, probably looking for their mail, and the little girl was just chasing her little ball.

I remember when my own little girl Christy came to see me at a house I was building. Her mother opened the door for her to get her out of the truck. She was only about five years old, and as I walked up, she looked at me and said, "Look, Dad, at my make muck." She is so precious to me. I just couldn't imagine that being my little girl who had gotten killed just playing in the yard with her little ball.

We still have horse and buggies here in Kentucky. Just the other day, an Amish family lost their lives in a stream when the lady thought it would be okay to cross with her children. She was rushing to get back home to get out of the storm. The whole family died except for the dad, who was working to care for his family.

When tragedy strikes, it can strike anyone, anywhere, and at any time. I know a pastor who lost his grandson in a car wreck. His grandson was in college to be a preacher, and everyone in the car lived except for him. Who knew these things would happen? If only someone could have told them, "Hey, today you are going to die." Do you think they would have listened? We all like to make excuses, to say *well, that happened because she did this or that.* Sometimes we put ourselves in harm's way. I've said it once, and I'll say it again: I am not going to jump in the water with a shark, yet we live in a world full of all kinds of evils way worse than any shark. At least with the sharks, you have a chance, but that's not so with Satan. He will not give up on trying to destroy you. He would like you to think God hates you and is causing you all of these problems. Satan will tell you, "If God loves you so much, why doesn't he do something?"

I remember one time when I was a teenager. I was lying under the car on the ground in our yard. It was a Pontiac Firebird; I loved that car. Anyway, I was working on the exhaust and couldn't get the bolt to go into the head of the motor. My anger kept growing and growing until it was too late. I was good and mad. I came up out from under that car and looked up in the sky and said, "Why don't you help me?"

Well, after thinking about the way I spoke to God, I shouldn't have gotten back under that car. But God loves us, and he said to me in a soft way inside my head and heart, "I am and I have helped you." He said to me, "You have hands, don't you?"

Some of us take things like hands, legs, feet, and eyes for granted. I know of some people who have lost some part or parts of their body. Most people will not know what it is like to have lost some limb, and I have friends who have all their limbs but can't use them because they are paralyzed from the neck down. However, they don't blame God or fuss at him because they are handicapped. This one lady—and most of you know who she is—paints pictures using her teeth to hold the paintbrush. But the best pictures I think she ever painted are the pictures she paints with words about our God, Jesus Christ, our Lord and Savior.

As I said, our trials and tribulation will do one of two things: they will drive you to God or away from him. You will either blame him or praise him. God gave you free will; it is your choice and yours alone. God knows everything that will happen to you, and he knows just how you will react to those tragedies and losses. It's your choice whether to serve him or not, and it comes as no surprise to Him. If you are truthful to yourself, you know whether you have a personal relationship with him or not. He says his children hear his voice. God gives everybody a chance to be saved before they die.

The Bible tells us 2 Peter 3:9, "The Lord is not slack concerning his promise as some men count slackness, but is long suffering to us—ward not willing that any should perish but that all should come to repentance." And in Ezekiel 33:11, the Bible says, say unto them, As I live saith the Lord God I have no pleasure in the death of the wicked, but that the wicked turn from his way and live; turn ye turn ye from your evil ways." Each and every one of us came from God, and he loves us, as we will see in the chapters to come. My mother had to make a choice to live a life of sin or give it up to live an eternal life with Jesus Christ, our Lord and Savior. She chose Jesus, and I am happy for her. I will get to see her one day soon when Jesus says, "Okay, boy, get up here."

Satan Is Relentless!

ONCE I WAS SUBCONTRACTING MY CARPENTER services out to a large building supplier. I received the paperwork for an installation of a storm door. I called and set up an appointment to install his door the next day. They lived way back in the woods. Upon arrival, there wasn't anyone there except another contractor doing some work. So I asked for the owner, and of course he wasn't home. "He's gone to town," the contractor said. So I called and received no answer, even after trying many times. I finally got his wife on the phone, and she said, "I'll have him right there."

It was store policy that the owner had to be home during the installation process, so I decided to wait on him to return. As I waited, the other contractor and I started talking. He was a rough looking man with long hair, tattoos all over, and his rock music going. But appearances never stop me from trying to tell someone about Jesus Christ and what he has done for them. So as we talked, I asked God to help me witness to this man. So, you know me . . . here we went, and I popped the question: "Are you saved?"

"I don't believe in that religion bull!" he said.

"That's good! I don't either." He didn't expect me to say that. He was just sizing me up. See, most people get nervous when I start talking about God. I knew this guy was trying to make me mad, so I carried on and said, "I am not talking about religion. I am talking about being saved by the blood of Jesus Christ, which is a new way of life." I then asked, "Have you ever asked

Jesus Christ, the only begotten Son of God, into your heart, to forgive you of your sins?"

"No, I have not!" he answered. "I have argued with many preachers, and they never win this argument."

"I am not going to argue with you," I said. By this time he had his knife out and was walking back in forth. I said to him, "You know God loves you."

"No he doesn't," he said. "I am not trying to make you mad, but what I am going to say probably will."

"Okay," I said. "Go on."

"If there is a God, when I see him they will have to pull me off of his . . ." and he was not talking about a donkey.

I thought for a moment and then, looking this man right in his eyes, *you will not get to say one word.* I worked with this guy for over an hour. It seemed like only minutes. Then he said to me, "I wish I had your kind of faith."

"You can," I said to him. "Just ask God; just trust him. You know God loves you very much, and Satan hates you." and without any hesitation,

He told me that Satan didn't hate him. Then the owner pulled up in the yard. That was the end of our little talk. He was right. I lost that fight, and it seemed as if Satan still had him whipped. I had tried to help him anyway.

I met another man a few years later. I was going to give an estimate on doing some flooring. Upon arriving at his home, as I got to the door, I could hear him inside. He was a loud-spoken man and an old sailor. The first thing he did when he opened the door was size me up; he grabbed my hand, so I gave him a little squeeze. Then he grabbed my arm with his other hand. He said, "You're a big boy."

See, I am six foot two and weigh two hundred and seventy pounds, and I bench-press four hundred pounds. So as I squeezed his hand, I gave him a little smile; at this point, I had his attention.

I thought to myself, *This guy is not saved*, and boy was I right. He led me all over his house, showing me all kinds of things he had done, most of which wasn't finished. As we walked around, I thought to myself, *How will I ever get to witness to this man? He never shuts up.* Well, it was time for me to go, and I noticed my wife was talking to his wife outside. He had sat down in his chair and was quiet. I thought, *Okay, this is perfect.* I knew what was going on; God had caused peace to come into that house. So I got down on my knees and asked him if he was saved. I asked, "If you died today, what would happen to you?"

We talked and talked, and he was very hardheaded and hard hearted. I was getting nowhere. So I asked God, "What do you want me to say to this man?" As soon as I finished asking, God said, "Tell him."

I looked at that poor man and said, "God wants a personal relationship with you," and without missing a beat, he said, "No, he doesn't!"

I got up, walked out of that house, and never went back. I shook the dust off my feet. Later, in the truck, my wife told me that his wife had asked her what was taking so long. Yvonne, my wife, said, "He is talking to your husband about Jesus." She then told my wife, "He will not get anywhere with him; he doesn't believe in God."

God tells us in 1 Peter 5:8, "Be sober, be vigilant because your adversary the Devil as a roaring lion, walketh about, seeking whom he may devour." Satan had these two men, and that is a complete tragedy. That's a hard loss for me to take, to see men and women reject God because they have given themselves over to the Devil.

I have a nephew who asked me if he could come and live with me. I told him, "Let's take a walk." I knew I wasn't about to take this child into my house. I had two girls and my own son, and this kid was trouble. You could see it falling off of him as he walked. While we talked, I explained to him how it wouldn't work; his attitude would have to change, etc., as we finished our conversation, I told him, "Son, you are going to do one of two things: you will serve God or the Devil. You will serve one or the other; it is up to you. Choose this day whom you will serve." It was not too long after that that he got to stay five years in the state of Florida's prison system. My nephew was a loose gun and out of control. He was released and is out now, and all that seems to fall from him is rotten fruit. Even after five years, we are yet to see anything good come from that boy.

Matthew 7:17 says, "Even so every good tree bringth forth good fruit, but a corrupt tree bringth forth evil fruit." Satan would have you to believe God hates you and just wants to cause you harm. Look at what God says about you, "For I know the thoughts that I think toward you saith the Lord thought's of peace and not evil," (Jeremiah 29:11).

I saw a truck the other day, and on the back glass in big letters was the word *relentless*. God spoke to me and said, "That's what Satan is; he is relentless." So I wondered what that word really means. When I got home, I looked it up in my old 1884 KJV Bible, and found the word zeal, which means devoted to a purpose. Satan will never stop trying to kill you and cause you troubles, pain, and hardships. He will never have pity on you, and he will always seek to cause you to suffer and struggle. He is persistent in his desire to see you die and go to lake of fire with him. Too many times, he is successful in destroying humankind. We know that people will be in the lake of fire. As Isaiah 5:14 says, "Therefore hell hath enlarged herself, and opened her mouth without measure." And Revelation 20:14 says, "and death and hell were cast into the lake of fire."

In the garden after he had prayed, Jesus came to his disciples and found them sleeping. He said, "What could ye not watch with me one hour?" Too many of us are sleeping and need to wake up and see what Satan is doing to our brothers and sisters, mothers and fathers, wives and husbands, and children. Satan will destroy you if you let him. He hates you and always will.

Many of us try to hide our lifestyles. We act one way in public, when everyone can see us, but the truth comes out when we are in our homes, where we think no one can see us. What does God see you doing when you are alone? What about all of those thoughts you have? He knows all about them too. You can hide your secrets from other people, but you cannot hide them from God. God is *all knowing.* You have no secrets when it comes to God. You will stand before him one day, and everything you ever did will be made known—everything.

Satan will tell you, "Don't worry about all of that; you're not that bad. God understands! He won't hold those things against you." He'll tell you that you can't help the way you are made or that this is just the way things are. You might be thinking you'll say something like, "The Devil made me do it." Do you think that is going to work? Don't keep those things bottle up inside you. Tell God. He already knows you're a sinner; he just wants to hear you confess it to Him. Don't listen to Satan, that old Devil, when he tells you that God hates you. God doesn't hate you. He loves you, and he wants to see you come to him and get saved.

In Romans 8:39, Paul said, "Nothing shall be able to separate us from the love of God which is in Christ Jesus our Lord."

5

Does God Love Me?

IT IS EASY TO THINK GOD doesn't love you, that he doesn't care about what happens to you, when all around you is sufferings and pain. When it looks like the whole world is falling down on us, sometimes we find ourselves in a place where it seems as if we are all alone and have nowhere to turn; we think there is nothing we can do. Often all we want to do is die and just make it all go away! You hear that voice in your head saying, "You are no good," and too many times this leads to suicide.

But that is not the answer to the problem. Others turn to alcohol; they try to drink their problem away only to find out that it is still there, and others turn to sex, looking for love only to find out it doesn't fulfill that emptiness inside them. There are many ways we try to find happiness, only to be let down, and often we find that we have made things worse. In other words, these path's lead to lifelong addiction or to other kinds of evil.

In this world, it is easy to turn your back on God. Judas was a man who had walked with God, and yet he betrayed him for thirty pieces of silver (Matthew 27:3). I don't know what could have caused Judas to do such a thing. Maybe he had bills to pay or needed some kind of drug; maybe he thought he could give it to the poor. People justify their actions one way or the other. Whatever it was, it led to his demise: "And he cast down the pieces of silver in the temple and departed and went and hanged himself" (Matthew 27:5).

What a tragedy to have walked with God only to lose your life for thirty pieces of silver. The love of money is the root to all kinds of evil.

For Judas, his life was worth only thirty pieces of silver. What is your life worth? We think, *I would never do anything like that, especially if I had walked with God.* Yet the Holy Spirit is all around us, all the time, and sees everything we do. Still we turn our backs on him every day.

Peter said the same thing in Matthew 26:33: "Though all men shall be offended because of thee, yet will I never be offended." Later he found himself weeping because he had denied Jesus, the Son of the only living and true God. "And Peter remembered the words of Jesus which said unto him before the cock crows thou shalt deny me thrice and went out and wept bitterly" (Matthew 26:75). Many of us find ourselves weeping, but not because we have denied God. No, we weep because we are out of money or drugs, we want our children to behave, the wife or husband left, etc. Peter was a man of God, no doubt; yet even he succumbed to the pressures of this life. Who knows? Maybe he feared for his life.

I know one thing: God cares for his children. For example, Luke 22:31-32 tells us, "And the

Lord said Simon, Simon, behold Satan hath desired to have you, that he may sift you as wheat but I have prayed for thee that thy faith fail not and when thou are converted, strengthen thy brethren."

Many have doubt in God and feel as if he has left them to fend for themselves or has forsaken them. One of my favorite stories in the Bible is in the book of John:

> And after eight days again his disciples were within, and Thomas with them: then came Jesus the door being shut, and stood in the midst and said peace be unto you. then saith he to Thomas reach hither thy finger, and behold my hands; and reach hither thy hand, and thrust it into my side and be not faithless but believing and Thomas answered and said unto him My Lord and my God Jesus saith unto him, Thomas because thou hast seen me thou hast believed: blessed are they

that have not seen and yet believed and many other signs truly did Jesus in the presence of his disciples which are not written in this book: but these are written that ye might believe that Jesus is the Christ the Son of God; and that believing ye might have life through his name. (John20:26-31)

God indeed loves his creation; God loves each and every one of us, even though most will turn their backs on him and will not seek after him. Most people want to call on him or test him when things are going bad and forget about him when thing are going good. I will tell my kids from time to time, "You can't put God on the back burner and keep him on warm until you need him. You have to have him on the front burner and on high all the time." He will have first place in your life, or he will leave you to your own will, with your own strength, until you see you can't do it on your own. Don't put God out of your life; give him the lead, and you do the following, saying, "Yes, Lord, I love you more than my life, children, husband or wife, mother or father, etc." It's all God, or it's all nothing; that is just the way it is. We are nothing without God.

We were living in Florida for a few years, and one morning we got up and were getting the kids off to school before we went to work. Well, I should say my wife was getting the kids off to school—thank God for loving mothers. Anyway, my wife gave our son some cough medicine and sent him on his way. Not long after that, we were heading off to work ourselves. As we came around the curve in our driveway, I looked up at the kids and saw my son standing there; then, all of a sudden, he just fell down on the ground. Well, I thought my heart was going to fall out. I thought I was going to die. I raced up to him, picked him up, and off to the hospital we went. I was scared to death. *Not my son*, I thought. *God, please don't hurt him. Please help us.*

See how easy it is to blame God? God didn't do anything to this child he gave us. No, it was his mother. I am joking, but what happened was that the cough medicine combined with an empty stomach and a long driveway and a son in a hurry running up the hill gave him an intense rush of blood to his head, so he got dizzy and fell down. We all know there is a God, saved or lost, and it is God we turn to when things get thick and times get hard—at least I do.

I watch a TV program from time to time about people whose houses are in need of improvement of some kind, and professionals come in and accommodate them. Anyway, I hear them say all the time, "Oh my god!" I often wonder if they know what they are saying. I also will hear people on the street or at work say things like "goddamn"; my 1886 KJV says in 2nd Thessalonians 2:12 That they all might be damned who believed not the truth, but had pleasure in unrighteousness. That means to be condemned to endless punishment, God says in Matthew 12:36, "But I say unto you that every idle word that man shall speak they shall give an account thereof in the Day of Judgment, and in

Romans 14:12, we read, "Every one of us shall give an account of himself to God."

I wonder what would happen if mothers and fathers would say things like, "God loves you, dear son or daughter," or maybe say things like, "God bless you, my friend." I believe if we would honor God in our speech and life, he would bless our homes and our country. Maybe some of those demons would leave because they got tired of hearing good and pleasant speech coming out of our mouths. In other words, try to make them so miserable that they can't stand to be around you. God said in Luke 6:28, "Bless them that curse you and pray for them which spitefully use you."

Think of how much better this world would be if we would just do what God says to do. Love your enemies, bless them who curse you, do good to them who hate you, and pray for them who despitefully use you and persecute you. Does God love you? How many of us would give up anything dear to our hearts for God? Could you give up a child? That is what God did for you.

Romans 5:8 tells us, "But God commendeth his love toward us in that while we were yet sinners Christ died for us." So yes, God loves you. He gave up his only begotten Son for you, and that is more than we would do for him. The unsaved are the enemies of God. Their evil ways separate them from God. They speak evil of him when they don't even know him as their God or care what he thinks.

Why Do So Many People Hate God?

WHY DO SO MANY PEOPLE HATE God? The answer to this question is quite easy. How can people understand why God allows things to happen the way they do when they don't even know God? And then they try to come up with all kinds of theories to make sense out of their lives. The lost say things like, "If there is a God, why doesn't he do something about all the suffering in the world, or why doesn't he show up and reveal himself?"

I was watching a preacher on TV the other day, and he was telling a story about an atheist. The atheist was standing outside the gate of a meeting, protesting. He was challenging God by looking at his watch and saying, "If there is a God, you have one second to show up." Well of course God didn't show up, and I don't blame him. God actually showed his love toward that man by not showing up because if he had shown up, God would have had to cast him into the lake of fire. But now, because God is longsuffering, this man has another day to come to the truth only found in Jesus Christ, our Lord and Savior.

Most people don't understand that God is a God of wrath. Hebrews 12:29 says, "Our God is a consuming fire." Deuteronomy 4:24 says, "For the Lord thy God is a consuming fire even a jealous God." We see in the book of Numbers how God consumed Korah: "And then the children of Israel murmured against Moses and against Aaron and God's wrath went out from him to consume fourteen thousand an seven hundred" (Numbers 16:1–35).

Many have spoken evil against God, and it seems as if these blasphemes go unpunished. However, the children of God know what is coming, and it isn't going to go well for a lot of people who hate God. They will not change this fact; look with me at God's warning to humankind. If you have a Bible, go get it and turn to Revelation 20:1-15.

And the Devil that deceived them was cast into the lake of fire and brimstone, where the beast and false prophet are and shall be tormented day and night for ever and ever and I saw a great white throne, and him that sat on it, from whose face the earth and the heaven fled away; and there was found no place for them and I saw the dead small and great, standing before God and the books were opened: and another book was opened, which is the book of life: and the dead were judged out of those things which were written in the books according to their works and the sea gave up the dead which were in it; and death and hell delivered up the dead which were in them: and they were judged every man according to their works and death and hell was cast into the lake of fire. This is the second death and whosoever was not found written in the book of life was cast into the lake of fire.

God gives you two choices. You will serve him, or you will serve Satan. Those who serve Satan's agenda will suffer the same fate he does. God said in Jeremiah 4:4, "Circumcise yourselves to the Lord and take away the foreskins of your heart, ye men of Judah and inhabitants of Jerusalem: lest my fury come forth like fire and burn that none can quench it *because of the evil of your doing*" (emphasis added).

I have noticed in my few years here on this earth something about children. Children have a rebellious nature, and they have the self-will to become who they want to be. Sometimes they achieve their goals, and other times they fail. Some are overachievers, and others . . . well, let's just say the poor little things just can't help themselves; everything seems to be against them. I would say to that, yeah right. Some just need to work harder, and some just need to work. Some choose to work hard at one thing and forget about what is not important to them. In other words, the things they like, they do, which is what drives them to reach their hearts' desires.

Let's face it; most people don't have any desire to serve God. The problem with most people is that they just don't care about what God has to say. They don't care if God likes what they are doing or if he agrees with their lifestyles. Most are just concerned with the here and now. They don't think about what is going to come next; out of sight is out of mind. They don't want to hear about the Bible or anything about God. They tell you they don't believe in that stuff anyway. It doesn't matter if they believe it or not. That will not change the fact that God is real and that he will have to do something with them; it's heaven or the lake of fire. The lost are hoping they are right. Sadly enough, all the lost will die only to find out that they were wrong! God is always right. Why do so many people hate God? Because they are of rebellious spirits, and they have evil hearts hell-bent on disobeying God! And until they get saved, they will never understand why God does things the way He does. To better understand God, consult the following verses:

> As He saith also in O'see, I will call them my people, which were not my people; and her beloved which was not beloved and it shall come to pass that in the place where it was said unto them Ye are not my people; there shall they be called the children of God. (Romans 9:25)

> I will have mercy upon her that had not obtained mercy; and I will say to them which were not my people, Thou

art my people; and they shall say, Thou art my God. (Hosea 2:23)

For by grace are ye saved through faith; and that not of yourselves; it is the gift of God. (Ephesians 2:8)

Henceforth I call you not servants; for the servant knoweth not what his Lord doeth: but I have called you friends; for all things that I have heard of my Father I have made known unto you. (John 15: 15)

Is There Any Hope for Me?

IN JEREMIAH 29:11, GOD SAYS, "FOR I know the thoughts that I think toward you saith the Lord thoughts of peace and not evil to give you an expected end." *Is there any hope for me?* This is the most important question you could be asking yourself, and it's one I hope you will take very seriously. Your eternal soul depends on how you choose to respond to God's call to repent and be saved by calling on the name of Jesus Christ to be the Lord of your life. Some people think that God has chosen only some to go to heaven and some to hell, but we find in the book of Ezekiel 33:11 that the opposite is true: "Say unto them As I live, saith the Lord God *I have no pleasure in the death of the wicked* but that the wicked turn from his ways and live; turn ye, turn ye from your evil ways for why will ye die O house of Israel" (emphasis added).

I hear God pleading with the lost to repent of their evil ways and come unto him. Scriptures like 2 Peter 3:9 cry out to the lost, "The Lord is not slack concerning his promise as some men count slackness; but is longsuffering to us-ward, *not willing that any should perish,* but that all should come to repentance" (emphasis added).

One of the saddest things I can think of is that hell will have people in it, which is not what God intended. Matthew 25:41 "Then shall he say also unto them on his left hand. Depart from me ye cursed into everlasting fire *prepared for the Devil and his angels*" (emphasis added).

God clearly loves you. Nowhere in Scripture will you find that God hates you; you will find that God hates sin. So yes, there is hope for you. God has allowed you to be alive today and has been patient with you, but for how long? Only God knows how long he will give you to repent; only God knows how long he will put up with you. There is an old saying: don't put off to tomorrow what you should do today.

Luke 15:7 says, "I say unto you that likewise joy shall be in heaven over one sinner that repenteh, more than over ninety and nine just persons which need no repentance." And 1 Timothy 2:3 says, "For this is good and acceptable in the sight of God our Saviour; who will have all men to be saved and come to the knowledge of the truth." So the idea of God wanting to cast you in hell is just another lie that Satan has led some to believe. God has not predestinated you to hell. In fact, Romans 8:29 tells us, "God said for whom he did fore know he also did predestinate to be conformed to the image of his Son that he might be the first born among many brethren."

71

In this flesh, not one of us can be received into heaven. Our sin prohibits us from going to be with God. That is why we need a Savior. Predestinated for hell? Not so! Predestinated to be conformed to the image of Jesus Christ so you can go to heaven? Yes! God knew before he ever created the world and the rest of his creation. He loves us so much that he died in the flesh for our sins.

God knew some would call out to him while others would reject his great love and be lost. God could have created you to love him alone, but that isn't love. Look at it this way: I have a child, and I tell that child, "You have to love me," or maybe I try to make him love me by beating him. Will that make him love me? No, of course not. He might tell me he loves me, but inside his heart he really hates me. Fear is not love. What if I gave him everything he ever wanted: money, beauty, knowledge, and the whole world? Would that make him love me? Of course not. He might act like he loves me as long as I am giving him things. But as soon as I take them away, I would see that love turn to hate. God gave us free will; he gave us the freedom to choose good or evil.

Joshua 24:15 says, "And if it seems evil unto you to serve the Lord, choose you this day whom you will serve." Some people seem to think that there is something you can do to save yourself, which is a lie from Satan. Your good works in God's eyes are like filthy rags. You could never in your own strength gain God's favor. Ephesians 2:8-9 says, "For by grace are ye saved through faith and not of yourselves it is the gift of God not of works lest any man should boast." God provided Jesus Christ, God himself and he alone, to pay our sin debt in full. Jesus said on the cross "It is Finished," meaning the debt is paid in full for all who will ask. All we have to do is accept the gift. Just take it; he's right by your side, waiting to hear from your heart. I'll tell you a story I tell from time to time.

A young man got a job driving a big truck. One day his boss told him to go pick up a load and carry it across the country about fifteen hundred

miles or so to a small town. The young man
said, "I can't. I am going to spend time with my
family and friends." His boss said, "You will go,
or you will lose your job." So the young man said
to himself, *Well, I need this job, so I had better go.*
"Okay," he said to his boss. So he picked up the
load, and it was very heavy—almost too heavy
to carry that far. Nevertheless, he loaded it up
and set out on his way for that little town. He
traveled large roads, small roads, up mountains,
and around curves. It seemed as if it was taking a
lifetime to get there. All over the countryside he
traveled. But finally he saw the sign; it marked
the little town of Jerusalem. It was a little country
dirt road that seemed to go nowhere. The young
man said to himself, *I have come too far to turn
around now.* So he headed down that old country
dirt road, the longest road he had been on yet. It
seemed as if it would never end, and he was about
out of fuel. Finally he came up on a very old
wooden bridge and stopped. The town was just
across that old bridge. He got out of his truck and
started looking over that old bridge and thought,

There is no way this bridge will carry this load. I will surely fall through and perish in the fall. The young man said to himself, *I'll have to go back.* Then out of nowhere he heard a voice behind him say, "What's wrong, young man? You afraid of this old bridge? You think it can't hold you?"

The young man said yes. "Look at it," he explained, "there are old nails hanging out, it's leaning to one side, and look at all of those splits in the wood! And where did all that blood come from?"

The old man said, "Yes, you are right; it's old. I built it a long time ago. And yes, I shed a lot of blood doing it, about two thousand years ago. That bridge has been around a long time, and many have crossed it, and yes, many have turned around, too. But don't worry, son, it will hold you."

"Have you seen my load?" the young man said to the old man sitting on the rock. "If you knew all the troubles I have had, you wouldn't think I could cross. No, I'll have to find another way."

"There is no other way," the old man said. "This is the only way into the city, the New Jerusalem. You'll have to cross this old bridge if you are going in, young man."

"There has to be another way," the young man said.

"No," the old man said. "I built that city too, and I tell you there is no other way. I surrounded it by a large gulf, so anyone who would try to enter would have to cross over the way I made. No, you will have to come by the bridge." Then the old man said, "Maybe this will help you. The bridge is called Jesus Christ, the only Son of God; all you have to do is trust him and pray as you cross. He will do the rest. You will come by the blood, or you will not come at all. Jesus is the way, the truth, and the life."

Yes, there *is* hope for you. Only *one road* leads to heaven. That road is Jesus Christ. Following are several Bible quotations that will help you cross.

> For all have sinned and come short of
> the glory of God. (Romans 3:23)

For the wages of sin is death but the gift of God is eternal life through Jesus Christ our Lord. (Romans 6:23)

But God commedeth his love toward us in that while we were yet sinners, Christ died for us. (Romans 5:8)

Or despises thou the riches of his goodness and forbearance and long suffering not knowing that the goodness of God leadeth thee to repentance. (Romans 2:4)

That if thou shalt confess with thy mouth the Lord Jesus and shalt believe in thine heart that God hath raised him from the dead thou shalt be saved. (Romans 10:9)

For whosoever shall call upon the name of the Lord shall be saved. (Romans 10:13)

God tells you what you must do to come into his kingdom.

John 14:6
Jesus saith unto him I am the way the truth and the life no man cometh unto the father but by me.

John 8:24
I said therefore unto you that ye shall die in your sins for if ye believe not that I am he ye shall die in your sins.

John 10:3
I and my Father are one.

Because they reject Jesus Christ, they are cast out into the lake of fire. Yes, God loves you. But do you love God? Have you ever felt his love? Here are some key terms you should understand:

- **felt**—realized you're a sinner

- **abhor**—to hate yourself for the things you think, say, and do that are against God
- **confess**—to acknowledge your sins and ask Jesus Christ to forgive you
- **forsaken**—to have made a decision to trust and follow Jesus Christ.

And after all that I have done, God still loves me. Now I can have a new Life!

Bible References to Study

Article 1-A: God Is One

I believe and teach one God in three persons—
Father, Son, and Holy Spirit.

- **God is omnipresent** (Psalm 139:7-16;
  Jeremiah 23:23-24; Hebrews 4:13).
- **God is omniscient** (Proverbs 15:3, 15:11;
  Isaiah 46:8-10).
- **God is omnipotent** (Genesis 17:1; Job
  42:2; Jeremiah 32:17, 27; Matthew 19:26;
  Philippians 2:10).
- **God is immutable** (James 1:17; Malachi 3:6).
  God cannot change to the better since he

is absolutely perfect; neither can he change to the worse, for he is absolutely perfect. God's perfection prevents any change in his attributes. He can never be wiser, more holy, more just, more merciful, or more truthful, his plans and purposes will never change, and God will never change.

- **God is the Father** (Acts 17:28).
- **We are also his offspring** (John 1:12; James 1:18).
- **God is the Son** (John 3:16, 1:1-5, 8:24, 14:6, 11; Peter 1:17-18).
- **God is the Holy Spirit** (John 14:16-26, 16:7; Matthew 28:19; Acts 5:3-4).

God reveals himself to us as Father, Son, and Holy Spirit.

Article 1-B: God the Holy Spirit

I believe and teach that God the Holy Spirit is fully divine and eternal (Genesis 6:3; John 14:26, 15:26, 16:7).

- *The Holy Spirit* enables humankind to understand truth (1 Corinthians 2:10-16).
- *The Holy Spirit* inspired human beings to write the Holy Scriptures (2 Timothy 3:16; 2 Peter 1:20-21).
- *The Holy Spirit* convicts humankind of sin (John 16:8-11; Acts 2:37, 16:30).
- *The Holy Spirit* calls humankind to Jesus Christ and exalts Jesus Christ and gives regeneration to those who believe by faith (Titus 3:4-7; John 16:13-15). At the moment you believe by faith, the Holy Spirit baptizes every believer into the body of Jesus Christ and seals every believer unto the day of final redemption (1 Corinthians 12:13; Ephesians 1:13; 1 Corinthians 15:44-58).
- *The Holy Spirit* gives spiritual gifts by which every believer can serve God through his church (Ephesians 4:11-13). The presence of the Holy Spirit is the Christian's guarantee that God is the believer's Father and will bring every

believer into the fullness of his Son Jesus
Christ (1 Corinthians 6:19-20; 1 John
2:22-29; Romans 8:16).

Article 2

- I believe and teach that the sixty-six books
  of the King James Bible are the only true
  testimony to Jesus Christ, the only begotten
  Son of the Almighty God (John 3:16;
  Genesis 17:1-7; Luke 3:22; Matthew 17:5).
- I believe and teach that all Scripture is given
  by inspiration of Almighty God (2 Peter
  1:21). It is the perfect treasure of divine
  instruction of all humankind and is profitable
  for doctrine, for reproof, for correction, and
  for instruction in righteousness (2 Timothy
  3:16). It is the standard by which God will
  Judge all humankind.
- I believe and teach that God indicated
  to human authors as they penned their
  manuscripts; therefore I teach and believe
  that ever jot and tittle was God-breathed

and that the sixty-six books of the Bible are true and trustworthy in every minute detail (Matthew 5:18, 24:35; Isaiah 40:8; Jeremiah 36:28-32).

- I believe and teach that the Bible is God's revelation of Himself to humankind. His word is without any error. Therefore, you can and must stake your soul's eternal destiny upon its message about Jesus Christ (Romans 3:23, 6:23; John 3:16; Romans 10:9-15).

Article 3

- I believe and teach the deity of Jesus Christ, his virgin birth, his sinless humanity, his substitutionary death, his bodily resurrection, his ascension to heaven, and his personal coming again. It is my firm and clearly declared belief that Jesus Christ is fully God and fully man in one person. This is an essential element of my Christian faith. Jesus Christ declared this in John 8:58, John 8:24, and John 1:1-5. Who are we to rob God of his deity or deprive him of his sinless humanity? Jesus Christ is God and man in one person. Jesus was virgin born in Bethlehem of the Holy Spirit and Mary (Matthew 1:18-25; Luke 1:34-35). The Son of God who lived in all eternity was now beginning to bring about our salvation in the flesh. This miracle of his entrance into the world to save that which was lost is the gift of God (Matthew 18:11-14; Ephesians 2:8).

- I believe and teach the substitutionary death of Jesus Christ, the only begotten Son of Almighty God. By this, I mean that Jesus died on the cross as our substitute. He died in our place, even though he didn't deserve such a penalty (John 10:18). Death is the consequence of sin, but Jesus was completely without sin. You and I, on the other hand, are sinners (Romans 3:23). Yet he went to Calvary, giving his life freely for you and for me (Romans 4:25; 1 Peter 2:24). Don't you see? Jesus Christ took our place at Calvary. That is the good news, the Bible's message.

- I believe and teach the resurrection of Jesus Christ from the dead. Jesus was removed from the cross by the loving and caring hands of his followers and was laid in a tomb (Luke 24:6-7, 23:52-56). Jesus Christ was indeed three days in the tomb, as stated by Jesus Christ himself (Matthew 12:40, 27:63; Luke 24:7). I believe Jesus was buried and then rose again on the third day (1 Corinthians 15:3-4; Matthew 28:5-8). Not only do I believe in the resurrection from the dead, I also believe and teach that Jesus ascended into glory at the right hand of the Father (Luke 24:51; Acts 2:32-36; 1 Timothy 2:5; Hebrews 12:24). Jesus Christ ascended bodily into heaven, and he is coming again the same way *perhaps today* (Acts 1:11; Titus 2:13; 1 Thessalonians 4:16-17). We call this event the rapture.

- I believe and teach salvation by grace through faith. So basic is this truth to

Christianity that anyone who denied it could not really be called a Christian. I base this statement on two familiar verses from God's word: Ephesians 2:8-9 and Hebrew 11:6. Redemption can only come through the grace of God and the faith God gives us in Jesus Christ, our Lord (1 Peter 1:1-5; Romans 12:3; John 5:24; 1 Timothy 2:3-6). I firmly believe that no amount of effort on our part can merit one iota of God's favor; nothing apart from the work of Jesus Christ can gain us access into heaven (Acts 10:34-35; Romans 2:11; Ephesians 6:9; 2 Peter 3:9; Isaiah 64:6).

- I believe and teach that spiritual cleansing comes from the cleansing power of the blood of Jesus Christ. This alone can and will cleanse us from all sin for those who come to God by Jesus Christ (Hebrews 9:12-28; Revelation 1:5, 7:14; Romans 8:33-39). The blood of Jesus Christ cleanses us from all sins—past, present, and future—and his blood alone cleanses us from our daily walks' defilements of sin (1 John 1:6-9).

- I believe and teach obedience. The need of works after salvation is the gratitude one shows to prove what is good and acceptable and perfect to the will of God (Romans 12:2; Matthew 28:18-20). Though salvation is by grace through faith alone (Ephesians 2:8), after the blood of Jesus Christ has redeemed a child of God, that person can now live a godly life (Ephesians 2:10; Galatians 5:22-26). Remember, work cannot save you; only Jesus Christ can do that. It not a burden to serve the Lord; it is a joy (Matthew 11:28-30; Luke 17:15-19).

Article 4

I believe and teach the fact of a bodily resurrection in the Old Testament (Job 19:25-26). Job states yet in my flesh shall I see God. In the New Testament, Jesus Christ states in John 5:28-29, They that have done good, unto the resurrection of life and they that have done evil unto the resurrection of damnation. Other Scriptures support the resurrection as well (1 Corinthians 15:41-49; 1 Corinthians 15:51-53; 2 Corinthians 4:14; Philippians 3:20-21; 1 Thessalonians 5:9-10, 4:14-17).

1. The Bible discusses the resurrections of Old Testament saints (Matthew 27:52-53; Ephesians 4:8-10; Luke 23:42-43).

2. The Bible discusses the resurrections of New Testament saints (Revelation 20:4-6, 19:9-14; 1 Thessalonians 4:14-17; 1 Corinthians 15:51-53; Luke 23:42-43).

3. The Bible discusses the resurrections of the dead/unsaved (John 5:28-29). and in Revelation 20:11-15.

Article 5

I believe and teach the eternal body and soul.

- The eternal body is seen in 1 Thessalonians 4:17, 1 Corinthians 15:44-54, and Revelation 21:4.
- The eternal soul is seen in 2 Corinthians 5:6-8, Philippians 1:21-23, and 1 Thessalonians 4:14-17.
- The eternal state of the lost is seen in John 5:28-29 and Revelation 20:11-15.
- The eternal state of the saved is seen in John 5:28-29 and Revelation 21:1-7.

Other Scriptures that support the eternal body and soul are John 14:1-3 and Matthew 25:26-46.

Article 6

I believe and teach that there is one true church, the body of Jesus Christ, consisting of all believers, and I believe and teach the need for attending and supporting a Bible-believing local church. We must not depart from God's Word concerning the one true church. Many denominations claim to be the one true church (1 Corinthians 1:11-17).

- The church is universal (1 Corinthians 12:12-14).
- Jesus said he would build his one true *church*, not *churches* (Matthew 16:18; Ephesians 5:25; Hebrew 12:23).
- The one true church is a group of people called out from the world and belonging to the Lord Jesus Christ, who gave himself for the church (2 Corinthians 5:17-21; Galatians 1:4; Titus 2:12-14).
- The church is the body of Jesus Christ (Colossians 1:18).
- The church is the dwelling place of God's spirit (1 Corinthians 12:12-13; Ephesians 4:4-6).
- The church is commissioned to evangelize the world (Matthew 28:19-20).
- The church is to have order (Ephesians 4:11-32).
- The highest privilege and joy of the church is to glorify God (Romans 15:5-7; 2 Thessalonians 1:12; 1 Peter 4:11; John 4:23-24).

- The church is eternal (Ephesians 3:21; John 14:3-4; Revelation 19:1-9, 22:16-17).

Article 7

I believe and teach that soul winning, Bible study, and prayer cause a child of God to grow in the grace of God and develop into a mature Christian. One must study the Bible (2 Timothy 2:15; Proverbs 15:28; Acts 19:9-10; Luke 2:45-49; Deuteronomy 5:1; 2 Chronicles 17:7-9; Deuteronomy 6:5-7; Psalm 119:7; Acts 22:3; 2 Timothy 1:5, 3:15; Acts 2:42; Matthew 28:19-20; Hebrews 5:12; 1 Peter 2:2).

Christians are also commanded to evangelize (Matthew 28:19-20; Acts 1:8). If you are not sure of what God would have you to do to help reach the lost for his glory, why not stop right now and ask Jesus Christ, our Lord? Let your heartfelt concern for lost souls motivate you to do something to assist in the proclamation of the gospel (Acts 18:24-28, 9:5-6). As Paul asks in Acts 9:6, ask, "Lord what wilt thou have me to do?"

All Scripture is taken from the KJV.

About the Author

W.D. TAYLOR WAS BORN DECEMBER 5, 1968, in south Alabama. He is married and is the proud father of four children and the grandfather of six grandchildren. He often says his grandchildren are grand!

Taylor graduated summa cum laude from Bethany Divinity College and Seminary with a bachelor of arts in ministry. He also started Grace Community Bible fellowship.

It is Taylor's heart's desire to see as many as he can come to the truth only found in the Bible, that truth being that Jesus Christ is our Lord and Savior. He has been influenced by his father-in-law and mother-in-law, both of whom help him in his biblical studies.

The controversies over many Bible doctrines have caused many of God's friends to shy away from soul winning. This book is intended to show that we can't let Satan stop us in our fight for our brothers and sisters. This book is straightforward and is hard-hitting. God does love you.